SLICE OF *Gourmet*

Samira Ghani

Copyright © 2020 by Samira Ghani.

ISBN-978-1-6485-8510-4

All rights reserved. No part of this book may be reproduced or transmitted in any form or by any means, electronic or mechanical, including photocopying, recording, or by any information storage and retrieval system, without permission in writing from the copyright owner.

The views expressed in this work are solely those of the author and do not necessarily reflect the views of the publisher, and the publisher hereby disclaims any responsibility for them.

Matchstick Literary
1-888-306-8885
orders@matchliterary.com

Introduction

I have 3 amazing daughters, my eldest is 16, middle is 13, and youngest is 3, so as you can imagine it's sometimes hard to please everyone. I'm always working on something that at least two of them enjoy. Developing recipes has always been a passion of mine ever since I was little and it got me through quite a few rough times. Now as a blogger who has a growing Instagram account it provides me immense joy to share my passion with you all. I hope you enjoy some of my favorite recipes thus far and make sure to check me out @sliceofgourmet on Instagram and www.sliceofgourmet.com

[Slice of Gourmet](#)
[Celebrating each other, one meal, one recipe at a time.](#)

Slice of Gourmet is your one stop food blog site for great healthy recipes for all including instant pot versions. Looking for a quick bite, a full course meal or just appetizers and drinks look no further.

People ask me why I've chosen to share my recipes and my knowledge when I could sell them or keep them to myself. Well, the reason is it is truly heart wrenching and terrifying to see so much hate, intolerance and ignorance in the world today. I know I am not able to cure all that is wrong but I can spread love, raise people up and bring people together. After much thought, I decided to spread love in the best way that I know how. Through our universal love for good food. I will share weekly international recipes with a little background on the culture of the cuisines. My goal is by trying different cuisines and learning about their cultures we can make our world a little more close knit and learn how to love and embrace each other. The recipes are all free! It's my way to promote healthy living, diversify our palette and spread some positivity. Please join me in making our world just a little smaller and one where we embrace one another by celebrating both our similarities and differences. Please share my site with your friends and family -- let them join in the fun!

Khao Suey

Chicken:
2 lbs chicken cut in small pieces
4-5 onions sliced
1 can diced tomatoes
1.5 teaspoons turmeric
3 teaspoons garlic paste
2 teaspoons ginger paste
1.5 teaspoons cumin powder
2 teaspoons red chili powder or to taste
1 teaspoon garam masala

Method:
In a pan heat oil and add onions and when translucent add the garlic and tomatoes and all the spices. Let that cook for a few minutes and then add the chicken and stir well. Add a little water and let it cook on medium heat.

Spaghetti:
Boil till done and set aside

Curry:
1 tablespoon Garlic paste
2 teaspoons Mustard seeds
1/2 cup yogurt
3-4 tablespoons gram flour
2 cans coconut milk
3 cups water
2 curry leaves
2 dried red chilies
Salt to taste
1 teaspoon red chili powder
1/2 teaspoon turmeric

Method:
In a pan heat oil and when hot add curry leaves, mustard seeds & dried chilies. When I'm it turns color add the garlic and then the coconut milk. Blend the gram flour with the yogurt and add that to the coconut milk mixture. Now add your spices and let it simmer for 15 minutes

Toppings:
1 jalapeño finely chopped
1/2 bunch of cilantro chopped
8-10 pods of garlic finely sliced and fried
Fried onions
Chaat masala
Finely chopped potatoes fried or potato sticks
Fried spaghetti
Lemon wedges

First put your spaghetti in a bowl and drown in curry. Add chicken on top and garnish with all the toppings.

Ingredients:

3 lobster tails

2 avocados

8-10 cloves of roasted garlic

1/4 cup chopped parsley

1 teaspoon crushed red pepper

1 bell pepper diced

3 green onions chopped

Salt to taste

2 celery sticks diced

Juice of 1 lime

1 teaspoon smoked paprika

Method

Boil your lobster tails in salted water till it changes color and it's fully cooked but be careful not to overcook it. Remove the flesh from the tails and chop it up. Then add all the above ingredients and mix it up well. Your avocados will mash up and make it nice and creamy. You could add 1 teaspoon of mayonnaise if you'd like. Using a wooden spoon stir the mixture so it's creamy and mixed well. Squeeze a little more lime juice on it. Take your hotdog bun and toast it slightly and add desired amount of filling. Enjoy with a crisp salad. If you'd like to make it keto friendly. Skip the bun and add the filling to the tail that you removed the flesh from. Enjoy and take a pic and please do rate this recipe and let me know your thoughts @sliceofgourmet on Instagram

Chapli Kabab

- 1 lb Ground beef or chicken
- 2 teaspoon coriander seeds crushed
- 3 teaspoons cumin seed
- 1/2 teaspoon garam masala
- 2 teaspoons crushed red chilies
- 1 teaspoon Kashmiri red chili powder
- 1 teaspoon chat masala
- Salt to taste
- 1 teaspoon ginger paste
- 1 tablespoon garlic paste
- 2 teaspoons anardana (dried pomegranate seeds)
- 1 chopped onion
- 1 chopped jalapeño
- 1 chopped tomato
- 1 handful chopped cilantro
- 1 egg
- 1/4 cup Roasted gram flour
- 2 teaspoons ghee

Mix all the ingredients and form thin patties. Top with a thinly sliced tomato and shallow fry tomato side down. After about 4-5 minutes flip it to the other side. These should make about 12 chapli Kababs

Garnish your chapli Kababs with chopped mint and cilantro and thinly sliced onions

Take a picture and tag me @sliceofgourmet on Instagram

Mongolian Beef

Ingredients:
2 lbs thinly sliced beef
3/4 cup corn starch
1/4 cup soy sauce
2 tablespoons hoisin sauce
2 tablespoons garlic, chili bean paste
1 teaspoon oyster sauce
1 teaspoon chili oil
1 tablespoon sesame oil
1/2 cup brown sugar
1/4 cup rice vinegar
1/4 cup corn starch mixed with water to make a slurry
8-10 garlic pods sliced
1 finger of ginger thinly sliced
4-6 green onions sliced
1 jalapeño sliced lengthwise
Veggies of your choice (I used thinly sliced zucchini, carrots & broccoli)

Method:
Coat your beef with 3/4 cup cornstarch and make sure it's well coated. Let it rest for 1/2 hour in the fridge
In a wok heat some oil and shallow fry the beef till almost done. Make sure you don't over crowd your wok. Drain your beef on paper towels. Drain some of the oil out and leave about 2 tablespoons in the wok. Add you ginger and garlic and cook for a bit stirring well. Now add all the remaining ingredients except for the slurry and veggies. Mix well and add the veggies and beef. Coat them well and now add the slurry and cook till the beef is tender. Garnish with sesame seeds and serve with jasmin rice
Please take a picture and tag me. Your support means the world to me
XO

Rainbow Rice

Ingredients:

FOR THE BEEF:
1 lb lean ground beef
Salt to taste
1 teaspoon garam masala
1 teaspoon turmeric
1/2 teaspoon red chili powder

Method:
Boil till done and water evaporates

FOR THE CHUTNEY:

In a blender first blend 2 teaspoons cumin seed. Leave it in the blender and add 1 bunch cilantro, 1/2 cup dried, shredded coconut, juice of 1 lemon, salt to taste, 2 jalapeños and 2-3 tablespoons of water and blend till well puréed. Set aside

FOR THE RICE:

3 cups rice washed and divided into 2 parts Boil water and ass 1 tablespoon oil and when boiling add 1 teaspoon turmeric and salt and add 1 part of the rice and boil till cooked. Drain and set aside. Make sure you salt your rice. You now have yellow rice.

In another pan boil water with salt and oil when boiling add rice. Drain. Now add 1/2 the green chutney to the rice and mix well. Set aside. You now have green rice.

FOR THE POTATOES:

Take 3 potatoes and slice it. Fry till done and drain on paper towels. Add salt and red chili powder to it. Set aside

Brown Lentils:
You can either use the pre boiled ones from Trader Joe's or boil 1 cup in salted water till done. Drain and set aside

Slice colored peppers (optional)

FOR THE TOMATO CHUTNEY:

In a pan heat oil. When hot add 3-4 curry leaves when it crackles add 2 teaspoons of dark mustard seeds and 3 dried red chilies. When it's starts popping add 1 big can of crushed tomatoes or 6-8 tomatoes puréed. Now add 3 cloves of crushed garlic, salt to taste and red chili powder. Mix well. Add the juice of 1 lemon and cook on low flame till it's darkened in color and thickened. Set aside

TO ASSEMBLE:

In a clear Pyrex dish layer your yellow rice first and press it down gently. Next we add the ground beef. Press it down gently. Slice your colored sweet peppers and add it as your next layer. Your next layer is the lentils. Spread them out and press down gently. Now add the green rice and press down gently. Next layer is the fried potatoes. Press down. Next layer is your tomato chutney. Press down. Cover and bake for about 20 minutes in a medium oven 275. Take out and garnish with chopped cilantro.

Take a picture and don't forget to tag me. I love seeing your work and it really helps my page grow

Oatmeal Nutella Cookies

Ingredients:
1/2 cup butter
1/2 cup white sugar
1/2 cup brown sugar
1/2 teaspoon vanilla
1 egg
A pinch of salt
1/2 teaspoon baking soda
1 cup all purpose flour
1.5 cups quick oats
Cinnamon sugar to roll the cookies in. I use 1/4 teaspoon cinnamon powder and 2 teaspoons sugar and mix it well to make a light cinnamon sugar
1/4 cup or more Nutella (depending how much you fill in each)

Method:
In your mixer with your paddle attachment blend the sugars and butter for about 2 minutes then add the age and vanilla and blend again for another minute or 2. Then add all your dry ingredients.

Method:
Preheat your oven to 350.
Make small rounds and make an indent in them with your thumb. Fill with Nutella and cover with dough and form into a round ball. Roll in sugar (you can omit the cinnamon if you don't like that flavor)
Line your baking tray with parchment paper and set the 3 inches apart and bake till done about 7-9 minutes.
Remover from cookie sheet and onto a cooking rack. Enjoy. Take a picture and don't forget to tag me. XO

Shahi Biryani

Marinade for the chicken:

2 lbs chicken
6 teaspoons garlic paste
4 teaspoons ginger paste
1/2 cup yogurt
Juice of 1 lemon
1 teaspoon turmeric
1 teaspoon red chili powder
Salt to taste

Masala for the biryani:

7 teaspoons coriander seeds
3 teaspoons cumin seeds
7-8 dried red chilies
4 cardamom pods
1 cinnamon stick
8 cloves
1 black cardamom
1 teaspoon nutmeg
1 piece of mace
1 star anise
1 cup fried onions
1/2 cup cashews
2 teaspoons sesame seeds
1 pinch of saffron
Make a powder of all these. Now add 1 cup yogurt to the powder and make a paste.

For the potatoes.
Cut 3-4 potatoes into halves and fry. Drain on paper towels

How to cook the chicken:

Ingredients:
3-4 tbsp Oil
1 bay leaf 2-3 cardamoms
1 small cinnamon stick
3/4 cup fried onions
4 tomatoes chopped
2 green chilies finely chopped

In a pan heat 3-4 tablespoons of oil and add a bay leaf, 2-3 cardamoms, 1 cinnamon stick. When hot add 3/4 cup fried onions. Stir and add the chicken and cook on high flame for about 6-7 minutes. Then add 4 tomatoes crushed. Cook till the tomatoes and chopped green chilies get dissolved. Now add your potatoes. Lower the flame to medium and stir every few minutes till done.

Rice: 3 cups.
Wash your rice and soak in cool water for about 20 minutes

Boil water in a large pot and add salt, a cardamom pod, 2 cloves and oil. When the water comes to a rolling boil add your rice and cook til almost done about 7-8 minutes. Drain the rice and set aside.

In your serving dish layer the rice and cooked chicken. Start with a layer of rice and add the chicken mixture then add another layer of rice and then chicken and end with rice.

Now in a separate dish add 1/4 cup milk, 1 teaspoon ghee and a healthy pinch of saffron and microwave it for 20 seconds. Mix and drizzle over the top of the rice. Cover with foil and place in an oven that's preheated to 275 for about 20 minutes. Garnish with chopped cilantro and serve

Makloubeh

Seasoning for the rice:

2 cups rice

1 cup Egyptian rice

1 tsp cumin

1 tsp turmeric

4 tsp better than bullion vegetable paste

1 tsp all spice

1 tsp cardamom powder

2 lbs lean ground beef, lamb or chicken

2-3 tbsp Olive oil

All spice to taste

4-6 cloves of crushed garlic

2 tbsp tomato paste

Crushed red pepper to taste

Salt to taste

Juice of 1 lemon

1 bunch cilantro chopped fine

1 onion chopped

1 tsp cumin

Veggies:

Copped cauliflower

1 zucchini chopped

1 eggplant chopped

1 onion chopped

1 tomato sliced

3 cloves of garlic crushed

Salt and pepper to taste

2 tsp olive oil

Method:

In a sauté pan heat oil and sauté onions and garlic till translucent. Now add the ground meat and spices and cook for about 10 min add the tomato paste and cook for a few more minutes. Set aside

Boil 3 1/4 cups of water seasoned with everything under seasoning for rice. Boil till almost done. Set aside

Heat your cast iron skillet and add oil. Put your all veggies except the cauliflower in there. Cover and let it cook. In the meantime roast your cauliflower in the oven. Drizzle with olive oil, salt and pepper and bake till done. Now mix it with the other veggies and do not cover it. Cook for about 5 minutes more. Set aside

Now let's assemble the makloubeh. Grease a deep sauce pan with olive oil. Now slice

2-3 tomatoes and layer the bottom so that there's a nice layer of tomatoes covering the entire bottom of the pan. Season with salt and pepper. The next step is to spoon the meat gently over the tomatoes. Take a saucer or back of a serving spoon and pat it down so it's nice and packed. Now you add the veggies and again pack it down. The final layer is the rice. Layer that then pack it. Put it on medium heat and let it cook through and let the flavors marry. Now the final step, you add your serving plate to the top of the saucepan and flip it. Gently remove the saucepan and voila you have a delicious makloubeh. Garnish with cilantro and pomegranate kernels. Take a picture, spread the love and tag me

Peri Peri Rice Bowl

Ingredients for the chicken marinade:
1 lb boneless chicken breast cut in small pieces
1 tsp cumin seed
1 teaspoon turmeric
2 tablespoons olive oil
Juice of 1 lemon
1/2 teaspoon red chili powder
Salt to taste (the peri peri sauce is also salted)
1/2 cup peri peri sauce

Method:
I marinated it for about 2 hours the heated some olive oil in a pan and when it was hot I added 1 chopped onion and 5 pods of sliced garlic and when it was fragrant I added my chicken and cooked till it was done and most of the liquid had evaporated.
In the meantime I heated a piece of coal till it was red and added it to a tiny metal container with some oil and quickly shut the lid and let it smoke the chicken.

Ingredients for the salad
1 head of romaine lettuce finely cut
1 mini cucumber finely chopped
3 green onions finely chopped
1 avocado chopped
1/2 cup of frozen corn kernels
2 teaspoons Chile lime seasoning
Juice of 1 lime

The sauce for the chicken:
1/2 cup peri peri sauce
2 tablespoons mayonnaise Or you can use Greek yogurt to make it healthier. I do prefer the taste of the mayo one though. Once your chicken has cooled you toss it this sauce and set aside.

For the rice:
2 cups of rice
1 onion chopped
3 cloves of garlic thinly sliced
1 cup of dill finely chopped
Juice of 1 lime
1 potato chopped
Salt to taste
1 chicken cube
1 can of chickpeas drained and washed
1 teaspoon butter

Method:
In your instant pot hit sauté mode and add your butter. When hot add onions garlic a 1/4 of the chopped dill salt and cook till fragrant and the onions are translucent. Add your washed and

drained rice and potatoes and mix well. Add 2 cups of water and the chickpeas. Add another 1/4 of the dill to the water and stir. Turn off sauté mode and hit rice. Once it's done do a quick release and fluff with remaining dill and lime juice.

Assemble your bowl by layering the rice first. Then add the salads next you layer your chicken and top with chopped avocado and sprinkle with smoked paprika. Enjoy and please tag me when you make it. I really appreciate your remakes and it makes my day to get them xo 😗

Khajja

Ingredients:
1 cup flour
2.5 tablespoons of ghee
Pinch of cardamom powder
2-3 saffron threads
1/4 cup water

Method:
In a stand mixer mix the ghee and flour till mixed well. Now add the cardamom powder and water and form a nice dough. Let that rest for 5 minutes. In the meantime heat your oil on medium heat. You can also start your syrup now. Take 1.5 cups of sugar and 1/4 cup of water, a squeeze of lemon juice and a pinch of saffron and bring it to a boil turn the heat down to simmer. It should be a stickier type of sugar sauce. Now roll your dough out to a thin rectangle shape. Now cut those in strips and roll them and pinch the center. Pop them in the hot oil and fry till slightly deep golden brown. Once done put them in the sugar syrup and toss so it's coated well. Set on your serving plate and dust with crushed pistachios. Take a picture and do send me your thoughts @sliceofgourmet on Instagram

Velvet Chicken and Mixed Vegetable Stir fry

Ingredients:
1 lb chicken breast cut in pieces
1 egg white beaten
1 tablespoon cornstarch
1 red onion cut into wide pieces
8-10 cloves of crushed garlic
1 finger of crushed ginger
1 head of broccoli steamed
4 green onions chopped
2 jalapeños thinly sliced
1 sweet red pepper sliced
4 tablespoons soy sauce
2 tablespoons oil
2 teaspoons sesame oil
2 teaspoons chili oil
1 tablespoon hoisin sauce
1 tablespoon chili garlic sauce
1 tablespoon black bean paste
1 tablespoon oyster sauce
2 tablespoons rice vinegar
1 tablespoon honey

To velvet the chicken you will need to marinate the chicken in a beaten egg white, 1 tablespoon cornstarch and 2 teaspoons rice vinegar and salt. Make sure it's properly coated and let it rest in the fridge for 30 minutes then put the chicken in boiling water and cook till done. Drain and wash it and set it aside.

Now in your wok heat all the oils and add the onions, garlic and ginger cook for a few minutes then add all the sauces and then add the chicken and the veggies making sure it's all coated well. Now make a cornstarch slurry with 1 tablespoon cornstarch mixed in water and add that to your wok. Cook everything for a couple of minutes and turn off the stove. Garnish with sesame seeds and enjoy. Do send me your thoughts @sliceofgourmet on Instagram

Spicy Guava Mocktail

1 bottle guava juice
1 tbsp cumin roasted and slightly crushed
1 tsp chaat masala
2 tsp kasmirii red chili powder
1 healthy punch black salt
Juice of 1 lime
#traderjoes Chile lime seasoning
1 small bunch of mint leaves very finely chopped
1/2 bottle sprite

Mix all the ingredients together other than the cumin seeds and Chile lime seasoning. Add ice. Now cut a lime in half and run it around the rim of the glass. Take your #traderjoes Chile lime seasoning and pour on a small plate. Dip the rim of the cup you just ran the lime around into the Chile lime seasoning till it's well coated. Pour your drink in it. Garnish with roasted cumin and enjoy. Please help me continue to develop new and exciting recipes for you by tagging me at sliceofgourmet and sending me some Instagram love. Happy Cooking

Carrot Achar

1 bag shredded carrots from #traderjoes
4 tablespoons black mustard seeds (rai dana)
1 1/2 cup apple cider vinegar
7 Dry red chilies
1 inch piece of ginger
4-5 cloves of garlic
Salt to taste

Spread your carrots out on a paper towels and sprinkle with salt and let it sit there for a few hours

Wipe curry patta and let it sit out with the carrots.
Cut the green chilies in strips and also set out to dry with the carrots and curry leaves
In your nutribullet pulse the black mustard seeds (rai dana), apple cider vinegar,Dry red chilies, ginger,garlic& Salt. Mix in your carrots,chilies and curry leaves and cover your container and give it a really good shake. Place in the fridge and leave it overnight

Gulab Jamun Ice Cream

1 can evaporated milk
1 can condensed milk
1 pint whipping cream
3 slices whole wheat bread
1 tsp cardamom seeds crushed
A pinch of saffron
2 boxes #nanak gulab jamun
Rose petals and crushed pistachios for garnish

Method:
Mix all the ingredients except for the gulab jamun and garnishes in a food processor and purée it. Pour it into a Bundt cake pan. Cut up your Julian jamuns in medium sized pieces. Save 6 pieces for garnish. I cut the jamuns in fours. Now swirl them in ice cream mixture and freeze. To serve flip it on your desired serving dish and garnish with rose petals and whole gulab jamuns. Enjoy and please help me to create more recipes for you by tagging me and sharing some insta love. Enjoy life, it's delicious

Bhuttapakka (corn coconut curry)

2 cans Coconut milk
1 Lemon
1 large Onion
1 bunch Dhanya
2 jalapeños
6 cloves of Garlic
1 tsp Ginger crushed
Salt to taste
2 teaspoons turmeric
10-12 curry leaves
12 ears of corn that have been cut in half

Method:
Make masala by blending the
Onion
Dhanya
Jalapeños (you can reduce it to 1 pepper if you don't want it too spice)
garlic
Ginger
Set aside.

Heat oil and add curry leaves. Then add the masala you made. Cook it for a few minutes and then add the turmeric and salt. Cook it for a few minutes till the oil comes to the top. Now add the coconut milk and cook it for a few minutes till all the flavors are incorporated. Here's where you put in the ears of corn. Cook on medium heat till soft and well saturated in the curry. Take it off the stove and squeeze the juice of 1 lemon on it and stir. Garnish with chopped cilantro. Please take a picture and send it to me so I can see your amazing work. Happy Cooking. This dish is best served with Mandazi bread. www.sliceofgourmet.com/post/mandazi-african-donuts

Lebanese Chicken & Rice

Ingredients: 10 chicken drumsticks with the skin on
1/2 of a stick of butter
3 tablespoons olive oil
2 teaspoons paprika
1 teaspoon cumin powder
1 teaspoon coriander powder
1 teaspoon lime powder
1 teaspoon allspice
1/2 teaspoon cardamom powder
6 cloves of crushed garlic
1/2 teaspoon nutmeg
Salt to taste
Red pepper flakes to taste
Juice of 1/2 a lemon
1 onion sliced

Rice:
2 cups basmati rice washed
1 cup vermicelli
2 tsp butter or olive oil
1 cup chicken stock
1.5 cups water
Salt to taste

3 potatoes cut in small pieces

Method for the chicken:
Melt butter and add all the rest of the ingredients. Mix to make a paste. Rub all over the chicken and potatoes. Cover and bake at 375 till almost done. Take off the foil for the last 15 min to brown it nicely

Method for the rice:
Heat butter or oil on sauté mode in the instant pot. Add vermicelli and sauté till toasted add rice and salt. Sauté for a couple of minutes. Now add your chicken broth and water and stir. Cancel sauté mode and close the lid and press rice. Once ready do quick release and fluff. Serve with chicken and potatoes.

Greek Pizza

1 pkg dry active yeast
2 tsp sugar
1 cup warm water
2 1/2 cups flour
2-3 tbsp EVOO
1 1/2 tsp salt
1/2 cup corn meal

Method:
Dissolve the yeast in 1/2 cup water and sugar. Let it sit for 10 min till frothy on the top
In your kitchen aid add all the other ingredients and when the yeast is ready add that and use your dough hook to mix your dough.

Cover the dough and let it rise for about 45 min to an hour till it's about doubled. Then punch it down and form a ball and leave it for another 45 min.
Then sprinkle the corn meal on a clean surface and form your pizza crust. I like mine in an oval flat bread kind of shape. Oil your baking sheet put your crust on. Thinly slice tomatoes, add feta chunks, thinly slice red onion and sliced olives. Add this to the crust. Sprinkle with oregano and garlic salt and shred some kefaligraviera or Parmesan cheese if you cant find it and drizzle with olive oil. Bake till ready

Pound Cake

Ingredients:

4oz cream cheese

1/2 cup butter

3 eggs

1.5 cups sugar

1.5 cups flour

1/4 teaspoon baking soda

1 teaspoon vanilla

1/4 teaspoon salt

1/4 teaspoon almond essence

If you don't like almond you can skip that

Method:

Sift all the dry ingredients and set aside

Beat the butter, sugar and cream cheese till pale and creamy. It takes about 5 minutes with a stand mixer. Now add the eggs one at a time beating till incorporated each time. Now add the flour 1 tablespoon at a time. Lastly you add the essence. Pour into your prepared pan and then turn on the oven at 375 and put your cake in. Bake till done. It took me about 40 minutes. Every oven is different so bake till a man inserted knife comes out clean. Enjoy and please take a moment and rate this recipe and do share your thoughts with me @ sliceofgourmet when you do make it.

Chicken Souvlaki

Ingredients:
2 lbs boneless chicken thighs cut in pieces
12 small sweet peppers
2 onions
1/4 cup Olive oil
10 cloves of crushed garlic
2 teaspoons oregano
1 teaspoon thyme
Juice of 1 big lemon
2 teaspoons of mint
Wooden skewers
Salt and pepper to taste
Tzatziki (you can buy this from #trader joes) or you can make your own
Pita bread
Thickly sliced tomatoes

Method:
Marinate your chicken in the olive oil, garlic, salt, pepper, lemon juice, mint, thyme and oregano and set aside for as long as you can (I marinated it for 45 minutes)
Put your chicken on the skewers alternating chicken, sweet pepper and onion.
Heat your cast iron skillet and pour some olive oil it and add your skewers and grill till done. Now add your sliced tomatoes to the same skillet and let it char.

And now we assemble the souvlaki. Heat your pita bread with some olive oil. Next you spread your tzatziki and now you add your chicken peppers and onions and grilled tomato and roll it up.
This makes an awesome school lunch the next day! All you need to do is heat it up I. The toaster over before sending them off to school. Happy Cooking! Do t forget to tag me in your remakes

Tomato Chutney

8-10 ripe tomatoes
3 tablespoons oil
2 jalapeños
6-8 garlic pods
Salt to taste
Red chili powder to taste
8 curry leaves
2 dried red chilies
2 tablespoons black mustard seeds
Juice of 1/2 a lemon
1/2 teaspoon turmeric
2 teaspoons Kashmiri red chili powder

Method:
I'm a blender purée tomatoes, garlic and jalapeños
In a pan heat the oil. When hot add the curry leaves and black mustard seeds. When it sputters add the puréed tomatoes. Stir well. Now add the salt and the rest of the spices. Cook it on medium flame till it's reduced to half. When it's dark red and the oil comes to the top, turn off the heat and add the lemon juice.
Enjoy

Kulfi

3/4 of a gallon of whole milk
1 can of condensed milk
1 can table cream
1 cup milk powder
1/2 cup sugar or to taste
1/2 cup pistachio meal
1/2 cup cashew meal
1/2 cup almond meal
1 healthy pinch of saffron

1 pinch cardamom powder

Boil the milk, saffron, cardamom powder and sugar till it's reduced by half. Keep scraping the sides and mixing it in the milk. Now add the table cream, milk powder, and nut meals and cook till thick and creamy. About 15-20 more minutes. Let it cool then pour into your desired molds and freeze till solid.

Pot Roast

3 lbs beef for roasting
2 bay leaves
10-12 cloves of garlic
Montreal steak seasoning
2 tablespoons woostershire sauce
2 tablespoons mustard
1/2 teaspoon celery salt
Black pepper to taste
1 beef bouillon cube
3 carrots chopped
2 celery stalks chopped
3 potatoes quartered
1 onion chopped
1/2 stick butter
4 cups of water

Method:

In a heavy bottom pan melt the butter and throw in the garlic, and all the veggies. Rub your meat with Montreal steak seasoning and put on in the pan to sear. Make sure you sear on all sides. Crush the bullion and add 4 cups of water, the wostershire sauce and mustard. Cover and cook till it's done to your liking. When there's 20 minutes left chop up more carrots and put it in the pan. Let it cook in the juices. When done, let it sit for at least 15 minutes before slicing. And pour on the drippings on the sliced meat.

Easy Shrimp Scampi

Ingredients:

1 box of linguine

1/2 stick butter

3 tablespoons olive oil

4 cloves of crushed garlic

1-2 cloves of sliced garlic

Shaved Parmesan cheese

1/4 cup chopped parsley

Salt to taste

1 teaspoon crushed red pepper

1 bag of deveined, skinless wild shrimp

Method:

Boil pasta to box directions for al dente pasta and reserve 1/4 cup pasta water

In a large skillet melt butter and olive oil. Add garlic and salt and sauté till fragrant.

Now add the shrimp and cook till pink. Toss in the pasta and the reserved pasta water and let the flavors marry. (About 3-4 minutes) add about 1/4 cup of Parmesan cheese and the crushed red pepper and add in the parsley and toss. Set it in your serving dish and add shaved Parmesan and serve immediately. Do let me know your thoughts when you make this

Persian Chicken Over Buttered Saffron Rice

Ingredients for the marinade:

6-8 cloves of garlic
4 tablespoons olive oil
Salt to taste
White chili powder to taste
1 onion
1 healthy pinch of saffron
Juice of 1 large lemon

Purée all these ingredients and marinate 6-8 thinly sliced chicken breasts

Ingredients for the rice:
4 cups of basmati rice washed and soaked for 30 minutes in cold water
4 cups boiling water
1 stick of butter
2 healthy punches of saffron
1 chicken cube
Salt to taste

Method:
Take 1/2 stick of butter and the saffron and sauté the drained rice. Crush your chicken cube and add that and salt to taste. Now add 4 cups of boiling water and cook till done. Fluff your rice and cut up the other half stick of butter and mix it in. Set in serving dish. Now heat your cast iron skillet and add some olive oil and a little butter and grill your chicken. Later it on top of the rice. Now cut a few tomatoes in half a few green peppers and onions cut in quarters and grill it on the same pan. Place it on the side of the rice dish. Dust with sumac and enjoy. Do let me know your thoughts when you make this XO

Thai Red Curry

Ingredients:
2 chicken breast'scut in small pieces
1 red bell pepper chopped in pieces
1 yellow bell pepper chopped in pieces
2 jalapeños sliced (you can omit if you don't like it spicy)
1 onion chopped
2 teaspoons lemon grass
1 teaspoon brown sugar
1 teaspoon chili oil
2 teaspoons sesame oil
1 tablespoon fish sauce
4 tablespoons red curry paste (I use the maesri brand)
1 can coconut milk
1 finger ginger finely chopped
6-8 pods of garlic finely sliced
1 handful Thai Basil
1 can chopped baby corn

In a wok heat cooking oil (about 2-3 tablespoons) now add sesame oil and chili oil Sauté the ginger and garlic till fragrant. Now add the chicken and cook for about 5-7 minutes then add the veggies. Now add all the rest of the ingredients except coconut milk and cook till fragrant. Now add the coconut milk and let it simmer till the oil comes to the top.

Serve with jasmin rice

Don't forget to follow me on Instagram for more recipes

Chile Lime Shrimp Over Mexican Inspired Salad

3 avocados cubed
2 mini cucumbers cut into small pieces
1 romaine lettuce finely chopped
1 jalapeño finely chopped
1 red onion finely sliced
2 tomatoes chopped
3/4 cup cilantro finely chopped
1 cup frozen corn (I like the frozen roasted ones from Trader Joe's)
1 cup frozen peppers and onions (I like the grilled frozen ones from Trader Joe's)
2 teaspoons taco seasoning
Juice of 1 lime
1 tablespoon Chile lime seasoning
3 cloves of garlic thinly sliced
2 tablespoons butter
1/4 cup shredded cheese
20 wild caught shrimp deveined and cleaned

Method:
Marinate the shrimp in the taco seasoning and sliced garlic and set aside. Melt the butter in a skillet and add the shrimp and the sliced garlic. Be careful not to overcook it. The shrimp is ready when it's pink. In the meantime chop all the veggies and toss them in a bowl. Add the corn. Give your salad a good toss. In the same skillet you used to cook your shrimp add 1 cup of the roasted peppers and let the flavors marry. Add lime juice, Chile lime seasoning and 1 tablespoon olive oil and mix well. Add this to the salad and give it a good toss. Now sprinkle your cheese and add your shrimp. Enjoy and do t forget to show me some insta love

1 cub club crackers
1 cup butter
2 cups light brown sugar
1 cup graham cracker crumbs
3/4 cup heavy cream
1 cup milk chocolate
1/2 cup butterscotch chips
1/2 cup peanut butter

Line your on with parchment paper
Layer it with crackers
Melt brown sugar butter and graham crackers and heavy cream bring to a boil stirring constantly
Pour over the crackers and add another Layer of crackers then another layer of caramel
Now melt the chocolate chips, butterscotch and peanut butter together and pour over the caramel
Refrigerate till cold
Cut in squares and serve